So God said to me . . .

RICHARD ADAMS

So God said to me . . .

London EPWORTH PRESS

© Richard Adams 1978
First published 1978
by Epworth Press
All rights reserved

7162 0313 8

Enquiries should be addressed to
The Methodist Publishing House
Wellington Road
Wimbledon
London SW19 8EU
Printed in Great Britain by
The Garden City Press Limited
Letchworth, Hertfordshire SG6 1JS

Contents

These pieces were first broadcast in Anglia Television's late-night series 'Reflection'. The author is grateful to Anglia Television for permission to reproduce them in this book, together with some of the illustrations produced by their Graphics Department.

A Word of Thanks

So God said to me, 'I suppose you'll be writing acknowledge-ments.'

'What for?' I said. 'Acknowledgements are always so boring.'

'Well, write some un-boring ones,' he said. 'Who have you got to thank?'

So I made a list: there was Colin Riches who mentioned my name in the high places of the East Anglia Methodist District; Geoffrey Thackray Eddy, Chairman of the East Anglia Methodist District, who happened to be listening at the time, and whose approval of my first four scripts resulted in my appearance on Anglia Television; Peter Freeman, Chairman of Anglia Tele-vision's Panel of Religious Advisers, who gave his encouragement and a free lunch; David Whiting of Anglia Television's Graphics Department whose cartoon illustrations combined craftsmanship and wit; and Chris, Liz and Jon who endured my frequent absences while I caused sparks to fly from the typewriter.

'How about that?' I said.

And God said, 'You haven't put *me* in.'

'Sorry,' I said . . . And God.

'Last?' he queried.

'Why not?' I said. 'You know the old saying—The first shall be last and the last shall be first.'

'Hoist with my own petard,' he said. 'Ah well, I suppose it's better than nothing.'

Look Up, Look Down

I saw God the other day. I did really.

I just looked up and there he was, sitting on the edge of a cloud, dangling his legs.

I said, 'Hello, God, how are you?'

'Not so bad,' he said. 'How'd you know it was me?'

I said, 'Well, I just guessed, really. Seeing you sitting up there on a cloud—wasn't anyone else it could be.'

'Rubbish,' said God. 'Could've been anybody—spaceman, steeplejack, window-cleaner, lift-attendant—anybody with a head for heights.'

'Yes, but not just *sitting up there* on a cloud,' I said.

He was quiet for a minute—thinking. Then he moved round and propped himself up on his elbows and peered at me over the edge of the cloud.

'What else?' he said.

'Well, you look like God,' I said, 'with that old wrinkled face and long white beard. You're what I've always imagined you to be. Who else could you be?'

'Father Christmas,' he suggested.

'Don't be daft,' I said. 'Nobody believes in Father Christmas.'

'Does anyone believe in me?' he asked.

'Well,' I said, 'some do, some don't.'

So he asked, 'Those who do—what do they say?'

'They look at the world,' I said, 'and they see the beauty and order of nature, and they reckon it couldn't have happened by accident. Must be God.'

'I see,' said God. 'And those who don't?'

'They look at the world as well,' I told him. 'They look at war and human misery, homelessness, pollution. They reckon if God existed, it wouldn't happen.'

'I see,' said God. 'You know their trouble, don't you? It's not me they don't believe in, it's themselves. I mean to say—I've given them the power to put it right. They just won't use it.'

'What power's that?' I said.

'They know right from wrong,' he said. 'That's all they need.'

'Not willpower?' I asked.

'Ah,' he said, and I'm certain he winked at me. 'They have to ask for that.'

'Ask for it?'

'Well, I can't give it to them if they don't want it,' he said. 'It'd be like stepping in and clearing up the mess myself. I couldn't do that now, could I?'

'Why not?' I asked him.

'Well . . .' he said, and he winked again, and smiled. 'It'd leave 'em with nothing to do, wouldn't it. They'd have such an easy time of it, they *still* wouldn't believe in me.'

10

Then he disappeared, and I thought about what he had said, and I remembered the smile and the wink, and wondered if he was joking.

Suddenly, he came back. He stood on the cloud, his face like thunder. He cupped his hands, and he called out to the world below . . .

'BESIDES—IT'S YOUR MESS!'

11

Knees Bend

This great lump of plaster fell down from the front room ceiling. So there I was, down on my knees in the mess with a dustpan and brush.

When I looked up at the ceiling, there was God looking down at me through the hole.

'Thought I'd just drop in,' he said.

'I wish you hadn't landed quite so heavily,' I said.

He chuckled and lowered himself carefully through the hole. 'Fancy seeing you on your knees,' he said.

'Well, I'm not praying,' I told him.

God looked thoughtful for a minute. 'No,' he said. 'There aren't many go down on their knees to do it these days.'

'They haven't the time,' I said.

'Plenty of time,' said God. 'Plenty of time. I know one fellow, prays quite regularly, all the way up the A1 at the wheel of his lorry.'

'You're joking,' I said.

And God said, 'No I'm not. I'm serious. There's a lot of things he gets sorted out between Hatfield and Gateshead.'

'I wouldn't call that praying,' I said.

'No, you wouldn't,' he said. 'You think you know what praying is. You think you invented it. Well, you didn't. . . .'

He stopped for a second or two, but I could tell he hadn't finished, so I went on picking up chunks of plaster and listening.

'I know your sort of praying,' he went on. 'Gabblers, grabbers and groaners.'

'What do you mean?' I asked him.

'You pray because you like the sound of your own voices. For all the sense it makes, you might as well recite the Bible backwards; or you pray because you want something, or because you're in trouble.'

'Come off it,' I said. 'We're not all like that.'

'Well, there's a few,' he admitted. 'Some who are grateful, and some in need; but they don't have to put it into words. It shows in their faces.'

I was horrified. 'Do you mean people have been praying all these years and it's been a complete waste of time?'

'I wouldn't say that,' said God. 'It's not a bad habit for setting your thoughts in order and deciding what to do—as long as it's not an excuse for putting off something that badly wants doing, or salving your conscience by thinking you can have a good pray about something and leave the rest to me.'

'But you're *God*,' I said.

'Listen,' he said, and he looked at me hard through the dust that was still spinning in the sunlight and settling on the carpet; 'you know I've got things organized down here, even if you don't know

14

all the ins and outs. You know I wouldn't tamper with the works, whatever people prayed for.'

I stared at him for a full minute, plucking up courage. Then I said, 'I don't believe you even listen!'

'Don't shout at me,' he said. 'I'm not deaf. But I don't need to listen . . . I *know*.'

Just Good Friends

This middle-aged woman with headscarf and glasses almost attacked me at the Jumble Sale. She trapped me in a corner near the shoe stall.

'You need taking down a peg or two,' she said. 'Saying things like that about God—drawing him sitting on a cloud like a funny old man, and crawling through a hole in the ceiling. It's not proper.'

I must admit, it worried me a bit. I was hanging about afterwards, waiting for a man to come with a van to collect the leftovers. I was thinking over what she'd said, when God came in. He knocked at the door.

17

'Come in,' I said. 'There's no need to knock.'

'I like to be polite,' he said.

'That's just what I wanted to talk to you about,' I told him.

'What's that?'

'Hallowed be thy name.'

'I've heard that before, somewhere,' said God. 'What's it mean?'

'Don't ask me,' I said. 'You're God. You know.'

'So they say,' he answered. 'Still, you say it more often than I do. You explain it to me. You do it so well.'

'Flattery,' I said, 'will get you nowhere.' But I told him the problem. 'If I go on talking about you the way I do,' I said, 'folks'll think I'm doing you down.'

'Selling me cheap, like somebody's jumble? You couldn't,' he said, 'I'm too big.'

'It's not you I'm worried about,' I said. 'It's what folks think.'

'Of me, or you?'

'You, of course.'

'Are you sure?'

After a while, I said, 'No.' I wasn't.

God sat down with a serious expression on his face and looked at me across the empty table.

'You think people will find *you* offensive,' he said. It was a painful accusation because it was true.

'Do I offend you?' I said. I really wanted to know.

'Do you think I'd be here if you offended me?'

With God sitting there, it wasn't so easy to repeat the usual answer, but at last I said, 'Yes.'

Perhaps I imagined the flicker of surprise that crossed his face when I said it. I couldn't be sure.

'You're my friend,' I said.

'Then you've answered your own question, haven't you?'

I said, 'Have I?'

'Why do you talk about me,' asked God, 'just as you'd talk about anyone else?'

'That's easy,' I said, 'I want to bring you down to earth—make you more approachable.'

18

'Like a friend?'

'Yes,' I said, 'like a friend.'

'For the same reason,' he said, 'that many people look at the man Jesus and feel they can approach me through him?'

'You could put it like that, I suppose.'

'I *have* put it like that,' he said.

'But I wouldn't want to be rude. Not to a friend. Not to someone really close.'

'If they're that close, you couldn't be,' he said.

'How's that, then?'

'Well, think about it,' he said. 'You can say things to a friend you wouldn't dream of saying to anyone else, can't you?'

'Er . . .'

'Course you can,' he went on, 'You can be honest with friends, rude even, 'cos you know they'll never take offence.'

'I suppose you're right,' I said, 'but folks put up barriers, don't they?'

'Don't *you*?' he asked.

'I don't know,' I said, 'do I?'

'Calling people Lord, Sir, Mister; using their surnames instead of their Christian names. What about that?'

I think I understood more than I was ready to accept. Habits die hard. I said, 'Yes, Lord.'

But he'd gone, as though I'd frightened him away.

Love . . . and Kisses?

I was taking a short cut through the churchyard where the old man was sweeping up confetti. I stopped when I saw who it was.

'Hello, Gŏd,' I said, 'I nearly didn't recognize you.'

'It happens all the time,' he said. 'Some folks don't even notice.'

'Perhaps they don't know what they're looking for,' I said.

'Do you?' said God.

'I thought I did,' I told him. 'I must admit it gave me a bit of a shock to see you sweeping up confetti.'

'I like to make myself useful,' he said. 'What's it for, anyway?

Trying to catch me out again, I thought. 'You know what it's for,' I said. 'There's been a wedding.'

'Oh yes,' he said, 'what's that?'

I tell you, I sometimes find him quite as exasperating as a human—or maybe it's because I object to explaining things I've never questioned.

'You know very well what it is,' I protested.

'One of your man-made ceremonies,' he said.

'Ordained by God,' I reminded him.

21

'Who says so?'

'I say so.'

'It's facts I want, not opinion,' he said. 'Who says I ordained it?'

I tried again. 'The Prayer Book.'

'Rubbish,' said God.

'The Bible then.'

'Rubbish,' he said again.

I said, 'God, you are being cantankerous.'

'No,' he said, 'I am being realistic.'

There was only one answer to that. 'Say what you like,' I told him, 'I *believe* you ordained marriage.'

'Even I can't argue with that,' he answered. 'Anyway, suppose I did. What for?'

'Reproduction,' I said. 'Bring forth and multiply!'

'Don't quote the Bible at me,' he said. 'If a reason's good enough, it'll stand up on its own.'

'Re-pro-duction, full stop,' I said.

'There's a lot of that goes on without marriage,' he said.

I studied him hard as he swept some confetti into a neat pile at his feet. Sometimes I could tell if he was being deliberately provocative, but not this time.

I offered an alternative: 'Comfort and companionship.'

'You're getting warmer,' he said, 'but you've got it the wrong way round, haven't you?'

I said, 'Have I?'

'If I'd invented marriage,' he said, 'it would be successful. It isn't always, is it?'

I had to admit it. I sometimes think there's as much immorality inside marriage as outside. Going through a ceremony doesn't make people behave any better towards one another.

God was reading my thoughts.

'Immorality?' he asked. 'That's another of your man-made ideas. Don't you mean a lack of love?'

'I suppose I do,' I said.

'That's one thing I did invent,' he said. 'Love. The rest all follows from that—comfort, companionship, loyalty. . . .'

'And reproduction?' I added.

'There's a difference,' he said, 'between love and instinct.'

'You invented *that* as well,' I protested.

'Quite right,' he said, 'but I invented one to rule the other.'

'Like a broom,' I suggested, 'to tame this stray confetti?'

'You might say that,' he replied. But he did not smile when he saw that, while we'd been talking, the breeze had scattered the pile he had made, and he would have to start all over again.

Tried and Trusted

I fancied an apricot yoghurt the other day, so I nipped into the supermarket on the way home. I don't know if God fancies apricot yoghurt, but there he was, standing by the deep-freeze.

'Stocking up?' I said.

'Not me,' he said. 'I've got all I want.'

'What are you doing in a supermarket, then?' I asked.

'I like to see what folks are up to,' he said. 'They think I'm not interested, but I am.'

'I never doubted it for a minute,' I said, but he gave me one of his special looks. Made me think. Was it honest praise, or was I just

buttering him up? I tell you, you can get into the habit of saying the right thing without really meaning it.

'There's a lot of habits about,' said God. 'It's catching.'

Reading my thoughts again.

'Such as?' I asked him.

'Where's your wire basket?' he said.

'Wire basket? I didn't pick one up, did I?'

'That just shows who does most of the shopping,' he said. 'Now, if your wife came in, she'd pick one up automatically. Habit.'

'I only wanted *one yoghurt*,' I said.

'You're supposed to have a wire basket,' said God. 'It says so at the door—"Customers Are Kindly Requested To Use A Wire Basket For Their Purchases".'

The way he said it, it sounded like the eleventh commandment.

'*Requested*,' I said, 'only *requested*.'

'You know what that really means, don't you?' he said.

'I suppose so,' I said. 'More like the eighth commandment. If I'm wandering about in here without a wire basket, they'll think I've nicked something. Nobody trusts anybody these days.'

'That's precisely the habit I'm talking about,' said God.

'But you can't trust anybody, can you?' I said. 'You rely on someone—he lets you down. You let somebody into your confidence—he takes advantage of you. There's only one person you can really trust, and that's yourself.'

God looked hurt. 'Not even me?' he asked.

'Oh, I know,' I said. ' "Trust ye the Lord And Ye Shall Have Pennies From Heaven". That's all a bit too vague for me.'

'You do *believe* in me?' said God.

'Well, of course I do,' I told him. 'But if I trusted you for everything in this life it'd be like opting out of it. If you look after everything, what is there for *me* to do?'

'Don't make it sound like a take-over bid,' he said. 'It works both

27

ways. Whose world is it, anyway?'

Fancy God asking a question like that. 'Well,' I said, 'it's yours, of course.'

'Precisely,' he said. 'I may trust you with the running of it, but in the end the responsibility is mine.'

'Then we're back where we started,' I said.

'Rubbish,' God said. 'Trusting *you* doesn't mean that I disown responsibility. Trusting people means giving them the freedom to use their own initiative, but being prepared to carry the can if things go wrong.'

Light began to dawn—I think. 'There's a difference, is there,' I said, 'between delegating and disowning responsibility?'

'What do *you* think?' he said.

I said, 'I think you're crackers, trusting us.'

'Well, there isn't anybody else, is there?' said God. 'Besides, there's no merit in trusting folks you can rely on. That's not trust, that's certainty.'

'I'd call it reliability,' I answered.

'Call it what you like,' he said, 'you'll trust nobody properly until you're willing to be let down, to build other folks up by risking your own downfall.'

'I can just see the supermarket manager working on that principle,' I said.

'So can I,' said God . . . but he meant it!

Cutting Remarks

There are never many folks in the barber's on Tuesday afternoon, so I went. I can't bear the hanging about when there's a queue.

'How would you like it, sir?' the man said as I sat in the chair.

When I looked in the mirror, I saw it was God standing behind me with a comb and a pair of scissors.

'You turn up in some funny places,' I said.

'This is the place to *be*,' he said. 'It's where it's all happening.'

'What is?' I said. There wasn't another soul in the shop.

'Ah, but you should be here on a Saturday,' he said. 'Football, racing, politics, education, television, sex. . . .'

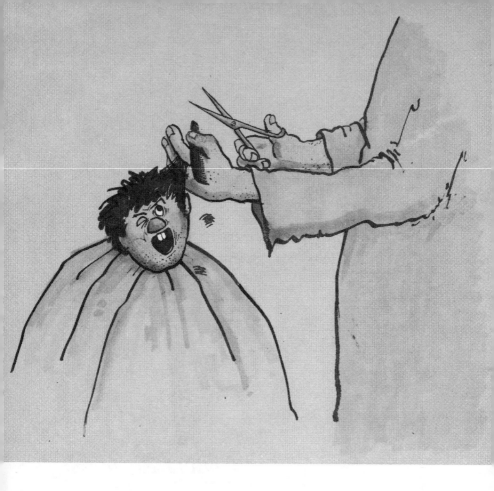

'All happening?' I said. 'The mind boggles.'

'Well, not exactly *happening*,' he assured me, 'but that's what they all talk about while they're waiting.'

'Don't you mind?' I asked him.

'Mind?' he said. 'Why should I mind?'

'Well, doesn't it get a bit . . . well . . . vulgar, sometimes?'

'Who are you to say what's vulgar?' he said, and tugged at my hair with the comb. 'I'll just thin this bit for you,' he said.

'Well, I don't want to tread on your toes,' I said, 'but somebody has to set standards of behaviour. You know the way people

30

talk, and the *language* they use sometimes. It's not fit for decent people's ears.'

'Who's decent?' he said. 'Are *you*?'

I didn't answer that.

'You know what I'm getting at,' I told him. 'Take that lot, for instance.'

Just by the door there was a pile of magazines on a table, full of glossy nudes, all bum and bosom.

'Naked as Nature intended,' said God, and grinned at me in the mirror.

'You're pulling my leg,' I said.

'They're just the way I made them,' he said.

'Then they're not offensive?' I asked him.

'People wouldn't think their own bodies were offensive if they looked at themselves in a mirror, would they? Why should anyone else's be? I don't know what all the fuss is about.'

'Yes you do,' I said. 'You're God.'

'All right,' he said, 'I'll tell you. There's bound to be argument, as long as there's one set of folks who think they know what's right, and try to impose their fears and fancies on other people—and the other lot who think that anything goes as long as it doesn't hurt them.'

I thought about that for a long time while he snipped away with the scissors. I couldn't decide who was more selfish.

I said, 'God, can't *you tell us* how far we should go?'

'No, I can't', he said. 'You'd want a different rule for every occasion. You'd never remember them all.'

'Well, give us a clue of some sort,' I said.

'I shall have to quote the Bible,' he said. 'Can you bear it?'

'Just this once,' I said.

'Jesus said it,' he went on, ' "Whosoever shall offend one of these little ones who believes in me, it is better that a millstone were hanged about his neck and he were cast into the sea." '

'But how do you know when you've committed an offence?' I asked him. 'Some folks hurt more easily than others.'

'Getting hurt,' he said, 'is part of growing up.'

Now I couldn't argue with that, but I wasn't with him all the way.

'But it can't be *right* to hurt people,' I protested.

'Not deliberately,' he said, 'but I'll forgive anyone who's honestly searching for happiness, and *accidentally* hurts someone else on the way.'

'Honestly searching,' I repeated.

'For happiness,' he said; 'without hurting anyone else, it takes some doing, but it's not impossible—as long as you don't mind getting hurt yourself.'

Dead Certainties

I went with my mother to Harry Burton's funeral.

'That's another one gone,' she said, as they lowered the coffin into the hole.

'Gone where?' I asked her.

'Well . . . I dunno,' she said, 'just . . . gone.'

When it was over, we made our way home.

'Seems such a waste,' I said. 'And Harry being so keen on recycling as well. He's got a garage full of old newspapers that'll have to be shifted now he's gone.'

'What *are* you talking about?' my mother asked.

'Old Harry,' I said, 'always in a hurry. If he'd only hung on until Saturday I'd have given him a hand with 'em.'

'Don't talk like that,' she said. 'Show a bit of respect for the dead.'

'Harry wouldn't mind,' I said. 'He's probably chuckling in his coffin right now.'

'You get worse as you get older,' she said. 'There's all his relations close behind us as well. Be quiet.'

'They said a lot worse than that about him when he was alive,' I reminded her. 'Never had a good word for him. What's so special now he's dead?'

She said, 'Shhh,' but I wouldn't.

'It's hypocrisy,' I said. 'They wished him dead when he was alive, and now he *has* gone they're making out how much they'll miss him, and expecting other folks to pay respects. Now why do you suppose that is?'

'God alone knows,' she said.

'Maybe he does,' I said. 'I'll go and ask him.'

'You'll what?' she began, but I was already on my way back to the churchyard.

God was still there, filling the hole with a shovel.

'Give us a hand,' he said. 'The regular fellow's gone sick.'

So we filled the hole together and patted the mound when we'd done.

'Poor old Harry,' I said.

'Why's that?' said God.

We stood our shovels sharply into the ground, and sat together on a bench looking out across the graves.

'They'll all be back at the house,' I said; 'drinking port wine and saying what a good bloke he was really.'

'Of course they will,' said God. 'Nobody ever remembers how good you were until you've gone.'

'He *was* a good bloke, though, wasn't he?' I said. 'He'll go to heaven, won't he?'

'Where d'you mean?' said God.

'Well, I thought you'd know that,' I said. 'That's why I asked.'

'About who?' said God.

I said, 'God, you're not listening—*Harry*!'

And God said, 'Harry's dead.'

I didn't know what to say, and I couldn't tell from God's face whether he was trying me out, or if he was serious.

'But what about. . . .'

'Life after death?' he said. 'No such thing.'

I was speechless.

'I know,' he said, 'it's what you Christians have had drummed into you, but there's no life *after* anything. There's just LIFE—going on all the time. I won't take away your beliefs if they're doing you

35

some good, but you mustn't make up fairy tales just to tickle your own fancies.'

I said, 'FAIRY TALES!'

'You look for heaven,' he said, 'and expect to find it at the end of things, when the so-called drudgery of this world is done. You think of life as a number of years of human existence. Who are you, that three score years and ten should stand for life itself?'

He stood up and leaned on his shovel, and he looked at me hard, and I couldn't look away.

And God said, 'When I put life into the heart of the universe before the beginning of time, I made it to last for ever. I created living cells in plants and animals, and the on-going process of evolution is simply Life itself, gathering momentum. Harry is part of the pattern. Oh, I know his body is lying there under six feet of earth, but the life that was in him goes on for ever. You can call that heaven if you like.'

'But I thought heaven was *real*,' I said.

'You want it to be real,' he said, 'to reward you for the good you think you do. That's no way to look at it. You're only out for what you can get.'

By this time I was desperate, I can tell you. I began to wish I'd never asked.

'Aren't I entitled to a little peace and happiness?' I asked. 'Isn't that what heaven is?'

'Of course it is,' said God. 'But it's no good looking for it in some distant, future Never Never Land. Look for it now.'

'Then tell me where,' I said. 'Tell me where.'

'You said yourself what a good bloke Harry Burton was,' said God, 'and how funny it was that folks were only saying good things about him now he'd gone.'

I said, 'What's that got to do with it?'

'It's true,' said God. 'The good that Harry did will never die. Goodness goes on for ever, too. That's heaven.'

'Brought down to earth,' I said.

With a bump.

A Real Dream

I'd had a rotten day. Arrived home to a cold, empty house, turned on the electric fire and, still in a wet raincoat, slumped into an armchair and sank into oblivion—wherever that is.

'Shall I put the kettle on?' asked God.

I opened one eye. 'How did you get in?' I asked him. 'Left the door open, did I?'

'Use your imagination,' he said.

So I did.

'Tea or coffee?' said God.

We drank instant coffee from mugs as the house grew a little warmer.

'Thanks,' I said. 'Nice of you to drop in.'

'I like to be useful,' he said. 'Must be the way I'm made.'

'I thought *you* were the Original,' I said. '*Who* made you?'

'Coo, that's an old one,' he said. 'You're not serious?'

I said, 'You can't take it seriously, can you—If God made the world, who made God, and if Somebody made God, who made the Somebody, and if Somebody made the Somebody, then who made the Somebody who made the. . . .

'Mmmmm,' God said, 'bit Morecambe and Wise, isn't it?'

'Logical, though,' I said.

'Too logical,' said God. 'Not enough imagination.'

'Go on then,' I said. 'Who *did* make God?'

He said, 'You did.'

I said, 'God, you'll get drummed out of the Brownies, saying things like that.'

'Do you mean Boy Scouts?' he said.

'I mean blasphemy,' I told him.

'Coming from *me*?' he said. 'Oh, I like that!'

'You don't mean we *invented* you?'

He raised his eyebrows. 'Don't I?' Then he added, 'Ever been up Everest?'

'I can't remember Eastern Counties ever doing that run.'

He chuckled. 'I've got my own transport,' he said.

So we went. The view was terrific, but I was glad I'd kept my coat on.

'I can see why climbers want to reach the top,' I said.

'Can you?' said God. 'They couldn't possibly know it's like this up here when they're down at the bottom.'

'But that's why they climb it, surely,' I said. 'Apart from the physical challenge—to compare imagination with reality.'

'To see,' said God, 'if their imaginations are telling them the truth.'

'You've got a thing about imagination today,' I said. 'What are you trying to say?'

40

'Try the moon,' he answered, and we stood there, looking down at earth.

'It was man's dream once to come here,' he said. 'Now it's reality; the impossible made possible.'

'That's not imagination,' I said. 'That's research, exploration, scientific calculation and human endeavour.'

'I'll swap you just one word for that lot,' said God. 'Vision.'

'You were talking,' I said, 'about *imagination*.'

'Vision,' he said, 'is imagination—plus the vital ingredient, purpose. It provides the power that enables men to think, to do, to dare, to conquer Everest, cure disease, harness energy, fly to the moon. . . .'

41

He'd have gone on for ever if I hadn't interrupted him.

'What you want me to believe,' I said, 'is that imagination is not just the stuff that dreams are made of, but the makings of reality.'

'Go on,' he said.

'And if so, then you—are not just a figment of my imagination. You are the beginning of what is *real*.'

He smiled, he grinned, he winked at me.

'Here,' he said, 'what do you think? ... who made imagination?

Breakdown

The car broke down—miles from anywhere. I had to walk a mile and a half to a phone box.

When I got back, the bonnet was up and a little yellow van was parked near by.

'That's prompt service,' I said, and the voice from under the bonnet broke into song:

'When in distress to hi . . . i . . . im I called, He . . . ee to . . . oo my re . . . e . . . es . . . cue came. . . .'

It was God, spanner in one hand, oily nuts and bolts in the other.

I said, 'What are you doing here?'

'Removing a fly from your carburettor,' he answered.

'I didn't know motor mechanics was in your line,' I said.

'Twenty-four-hour service,' he said. 'Breakdowns a speciality.'

'I've been wondering about that,' I said.

'What's that?' said God, screwing the nuts back on.

'The way you turn up in times of crisis.'

'Only time *to* turn up,' he said. 'Look at the way they all flocked back to church in the war.'

'That's what I mean,' I told him. 'It's a bit late to ask for help when they've started a crisis without it. They should have called you in in the first place to help prevent it.'

'Try her now,' he said, so I got in and started the car. Perfect.

'Cup o' tea?' I asked him.

'Don't mind if I do,' said God, and joined me in the car.

'You're not serious?' he asked.

'What about?' I said.

'Folks calling me in before the worst happens,' he said.

'Well, come on,' I said. 'You wouldn't want us to wait until things were beyond hope, would you?'

He started to mutter into his tea, 'The beginning of salvation is despair—who said that?' Then he said, 'No, not really. It's just that I'm getting used to it. Stands to reason nobody wants me when things are going well.'

'But that's not fair,' I said.

'It's only natural,' said God. 'They think they can manage on their own.'

So I said, 'But they can't, can they? You've heard them when things go wrong—What have I done to deserve this? they shout. They expect *you* to play fair.'

'No they don't,' he said. 'They don't expect me to be fair at all. They expect me to love them. They know my weakness all right.'

I said, 'Weakness?'

God said, 'Love.'

I was confused. 'I thought love was strength.'

'Maybe it is,' he said. 'But it isn't fair, is it? The nature of love is to give more than it gets. Still . . . I can afford it.'

I said, 'God, you worry me. Do you mean that people can do as they please? Ignore you? Forget you? Commit all sorts of crime and hypocrisy—and get away with it?'

He said, 'No. I can afford to love so freely because I've built fairness into the whole scheme of things. It looks after itself.'

I said, 'I don't believe it.'

44

He didn't seem surprised. 'I know it's hard,' he said. 'You think life's not fair becase you see folks getting hurt through no fault of their own, suffering from other men's sins. . . . You like driving?'

'Yes,' I said.

'Ever think of the risks you take every time you go out on the road?'

'No,' I said, 'I just get in and go.'

And God said, 'There you are, then. It's a risky business, living—exploring this world of mine, down mines, in forests, under the sea. I don't know why you bother.'

'Yes, you do,' I told him. 'We need the coal, timber, oil. If you will put it in awkward places, what else are we to do?'

'Go without,' he suggested.

'You don't really mean that,' I said. 'What about progress? What about a decent standard of living?'

'Well, you know what you're doing then, don't you,' said God. 'I don't know what you're moaning about.'

I began to wonder myself.

'Listen,' he went on. 'Sometimes you take a calculated risk. Yes?'

I nodded.

'And sometimes you have to experiment—take a leap in the dark. Yes?'

I could see he didn't expect me to contradict him, so I didn't try, but he must have thought I'd been quiet for too long.

'What about accidents?' he said, and waited for an answer.

'Mistakes?' I ventured. 'Irresponsibility? Ignorance?'

'Well done,' he said. 'You're not as daft as you look, are you?'

'Thanks,' I said.

'Then you say—"Ah, but . . .",' he added.

I said, 'Do I? But what . . . ?'

'But what about the innocent getting hurt?'

'Want *me* to answer that?' I said.

He smiled. 'Why not?'

So I had a go. 'No one,' I began, 'can escape the consequences of being free to use the world you've made. . . .'

'Or else. . . ?' he prompted.

'It would take responsibility away from us?'

'Nice try,' he said. 'Thanks for the tea.' He got out of the car. Then he asked, 'You want to share in this world's good things?'

'Of course.'

'And for the sake of progress, you're ready to take the risks involved?'

'I suppose so.'

'Then you're ready to accept your share of the world's afflictions,' he continued. 'Wouldn't you call that fair?'

'It may be fair for everyone else,' I snapped, 'but it doesn't seem fair for me.'

'That's just the point,' he answered. 'You want the world to revolve around *you*. You forget. It revolves around *me*, and you are only one small part of my entire creation. You can't even begin to understand your part in it.'

'Well, why don't you tell me,' I said, 'before it's too late?'

'Listen,' he said, and I don't know if he lifted the spanner as a threat or if he was simply gathering up his tools. He looked pretty fierce anyway. 'You'd like to understand the mind of God within your minute life-span? Let me tell you that what you look back

47

upon and call the history of mankind, is only the beginning of the history of God. You should know the *end* before I've hardly started? Who are *you*?'

When, at last, I found my voice, I said, 'Just an ordinary bloke. I can't even cope with a fly in my carburettor.'

God smiled and dropped the spanner into his tool-box. 'If you've any more trouble,' he said, 'just give me a call.'

Whose Move Next?

The removal men had gone for a cup of tea, but *someone* was thudding about upstairs.

I called up—'God. What are you doing up there?'

And God called back, 'It's this single wardrobe—it won't go down.'

We managed to shift it back into the bedroom.

'What about through the window?' I said.

'Too big,' said God.

I said, 'Too big? The window?'

If God had worn specs he'd have given me a very old-fashioned look over the top of them.

He did anyway. 'I'll get a screwdriver,' I said.

We laid the wardrobe on its side and took out all the screws we could find, but it was glued as well.

'We could ease off the sides with the screwdriver,' I suggested.

'Ruin a good wardrobe,' said God.

So we sat on the wardrobe, dangling our legs and searching the empty floorboards for a speck of inspiration.

'How'd you get it in?' asked God.

'It was here when we came,' I told him, 'a gift from the previous occupants.'

'They must have had the same trouble,' he said. 'How do you suppose *they* got it in?'

'Don't you know?' I said. 'I thought God knew everything.'

'Maybe I do, maybe I don't,' he said. 'Even if I do, that's not to say I'm telling, is it?'

'Now that's not fair,' I said. 'If faith can move mountains, it can move wardrobes.'

'How poetic,' said God. 'Say some more.'

I said, 'God, you are getting up my nose.'

'What a terrible place to be,' he said, but I ignored him.

'Don't you *do* miracles any more?' I asked him.

'All the time,' he said. 'All the time.'

'Well, do us one now,' I said. 'Do us a favour and put that wardrobe on the van.'

He was quiet for a minute. Then he got off the wardrobe and padded across to the door. He turned, and I caught the mischievous glint in his eye as he said, 'While I'm at it, I could transport the wardrobe across to the other side of the village and put it exactly where you want it in your new bungalow.

'You're not kidding?' I said.

50

'No,' said God. 'You get it down the stairs and I'll drive the van.'

I could see I wasn't going to get the sort of answer I wanted, so I followed him downstairs, and we sat in the garden observing the wonders of nature.

'See what I mean?' said God, pulling a daisy out of the lawn. 'Pick yourself a miracle.'

'Oh, I know about that,' I said. 'But it's not like the old days, is it?'

'You don't live in the old days,' he said.

'Well . . . I know,' I said. 'But what's happened to things like the pillar of fire in the desert, stilling storms, water into wine. . . ?'

'You know what I think,' said God. 'Folks were still growing in

51

those days. What they'd discovered they took the credit for. What they didn't understand they left to me—or cursed me for . . . a bit like you.'

I said, 'Haven't we grown up then?'

'Well . . .' he said, 'a little, I suppose, but not as much as you think. Your scientists and explorers are unearthing miracles all the time. But *who* gets the Queen's Award for Industry and the Nobel Prize? Me?'

I said, 'God, you're jealous. You think *we* take the credit for *your* miracles. Well maybe we don't think they *are* miracles.'

And God said, 'Just because you can explain them?'

52

'Well, I can't', I said, 'but scientists can. Anyway, that still leaves room for *real* miracles, doesn't it?'

So he said, 'Maybe it does. But I don't like being treated like the missing bits in a jigsaw puzzle. I'm the whole picture or nothing.'

So I told him straight. 'Maybe you're not the whole picture, then. Maybe you are nothing.'

Angry though he was, he showed no surprise at what I'd said, but he had his answer ready.

'You know what?' said God.

'What?'

'I can't think of a time when I wasn't part of man's quest for truth, meaning and purpose in life.'

'You want to think a bit harder, then,' I said.

'I don't have to *think*,' he answered. 'I *know*. You're the one that has to do the thinking, piecing together the religious jigsaw.'

'Pitting my wits against yours?' I said. 'What chance have I got?'

'Every chance,' he said. 'As long as you remember it's not just brainwork. You're body and spirit as well, you know. Put your whole self in . . .'

'Your whole self out, you do the hokey-cokey and you. . . .'

'I'm serious,' he interrupted. '*Your* whole self, *my* whole self. Make me responsible only for the bits of the puzzle that are missing, or say that I'm nothing to do with it, and you run the risk of never completing the puzzle at all.'

Missing the Bus

The car broke down again, so I had to take the bus.

A dark voice said, 'Where to?'

'Return to Northampton,' I said. And good-bye to another pound note.

Nobody else on the bus. Slack time of day.

'Vicious circle,' the bus conductor said, and sat down beside me. 'I'm only here for the ride, I reckon. Few more years, you'll be able to buy the bus for less than the fare to Rushden.'

The bus stops flicked by without stopping us.

'Don't I know you?' he said.

'Shouldn't think so,' I said. 'I don't live here any more.'

'Never forget a face,' he insisted. 'I've seen you somewhere.'

'I live in Norfolk now,' I told him.

'Ah,' he said, 'Anglia.'

'That's right,' I said, 'East Anglia.'

'No,' he said, 'Anglia Television. I see you on telly.'

'Well, just now and again,' I said.

'When I am on late shift,' he went on, 'I get home. You only thing left to watch on telly.'

'Except the Queen,' I said.

'You tell funny stories,' he said. 'Queen, not very funny.'

'Thanks,' I said.

'Your funny God-man in long white nightshirt,' he said, 'shifting wardrobes, making coffee—I saw them.'

'Nice to know somebody watches,' I said. 'I thought all decent folk had gone to bed by the time I was on.'

But he said, 'I ask myself—is that a way for a man to talk about his God?'

'It's just the way I see him,' I said. 'It brings him down to earth. I see him in ordinary people, I hear him in ordinary people. An everyday action, an everyday word, the hand or voice of God.'

'Why do you say *ordinary* people, then?' he asked. 'If God is in them . . . *extra*ordinary people. . . . You treat them special?'

I suddenly felt rather inadequate.

'I do my best,' I said. 'Like other people. But you can see why I make my God a caretaker, coffee-maker, removal man. . . .'

'And bus conductor?' he wanted to know.

'Maybe I'll get round to it,' I said. 'I hadn't thought about it.'

He looked disappointed, but the bus had drawn up at my stop.

'My God,' he said, 'has a black face.'

I got off the bus and stood on the pavement, wondering why I felt so deflated after such a pleasant conversation. Then, as the bus pulled away, I was startled to see a face grinning at me from the back step.

It was God—white nightshirt, white whiskers, white face—the strong, warm, wise Olde Englishe character I'd always imagined him to be.

I'd caught a bus . . . and missed one.

56

Clowning

They keep mucking about with the streets in the middle of the city.

One week, you leave the car park, turn right, straight down to Magdalen Street, turn left and you're on you're way home. Next week, leave the car park, turn right, twenty yards, dead end. No signs, no warning—four concrete bollards slap across the road.

So—into reverse, find another way home. Tap-tap on the car roof. Wind the window down. Guess who. . . ?

So I said, 'Hello, God.'

'Having trouble?' he asked.

'Bollards,' I said.

He said, 'I beg your pardon.'

'They weren't there last week,' I told him.

'Life's full of surprises,' he said. 'You must learn to live with the unexpected.'

'I'm only just getting used to having you popping up unannounced,' I said. 'Let me turn this car round.'

God stood on the pavement, smirking like an idiot while I did a ninety-point turn in the narrow road. That really made me mad, so I went for him.

'Sometimes I reckon all you ever do is laugh at all our human struggles and predicaments.'

'Don't shout,' said God. 'Folks are staring at you.'

'I don't care,' I said. 'Let 'em know the truth. You just made us for your own amusement so you could practise the pranks of nature on us and laugh at our discomfort. You're no more than a great big Clown in the Sky waiting to catch us with our pants down.'

'Fascinating,' said God. 'Folks keep saying I ought to change my image, but that's one I hadn't thought of. What's so wrong with being a clown anyway?'

I told him, 'It's humiliating.'

'Who for?' he said.

I said, 'What do you mean—who for? Who am I talking about?'

'People,' he said, 'with their pants down.'

I just wasn't getting through. I had to shout again to make him understand. 'I'm talking about *you*,' I said. 'You—God—exploiting our innocence, mocking our ignorance, laughing at us when we're down.'

He looked disappointed. 'You're not serious, are you?' he said. 'Do you really believe that? Have you never got up and dusted yourself down?'

I said, 'Well, I. . . .'

'Take just now,' he went on. 'You went one way—couldn't get, so you turn round and try another.'

'With a struggle,' I said.

'Won't you ever learn?' said God. 'That's how things are. It's the struggles that ram home the truth. It's striving and searching for answers that help you to grow as a person. . . . You won't go that way again, will you?'

'I wouldn't rely on it,' I said.

'There you go again,' he said. 'You know, the only reason you

accuse me of laughing at your misfortunes is because it makes a good excuse for your own defeatism. You do yourself down and then drag me down to keep you company. Well, of course, God's a clown if *you* are.'

'So we are made in God's image,' I said; rudely, I thought, but he didn't seem worried by it.

'Sounds to me,' he said, 'as though you think being human is a good excuse for failure.'

'Isn't it?' I asked.

'Silly question,' he answered. 'Of course it isn't. To be human is to have potential.'

He let me think about that for a while. Then he said, 'But you don't improve people by putting yourself on a pedestal. See me as a clown, do you? What you see is a reflection of your own folly. Didn't you recognize it?'

'Is that all?' I said.

'No, it isn't. Why do you suppose I choose to identify myself with human frailty and stupidity?'

He waited for an answer, but I hadn't got one ready.

'I want you to know,' he said, 'that I'm always ready to meet your needs, alleviate your anxieties. . . .'

And suddenly I found a word. It was, 'How?'

And God said, 'I share them and understand them.'

Was he hinting that I'd never be any good to other people unless I was prepared to put myself in their shoes?

I said, 'Are you trying to tell me that old story about the man Jesus whom some people say was God in human form?'

And he said, 'Please yourself. What use *is* divinity unless it can wear the shoes of humanity?'

'Even the shoes of a clown?' I said.

And God wrinkled his nose and said, 'Not shoes—BOOTS!'

Isms

Raining cats and dogs it was. And there he was, plodding back and forth along the pavements, knocked about by water-logged shoppers on a Saturday morning.

It was God. At least he'd had the sense to put a waterproof nightgown on. But there he was, parading his placard up and down and handing out soggy pamphlets to anyone with time enough to grab one.

'You look like a drowned rat,' I said to him. 'What do you think you're doing?'

'Spreading the Word,' he said.

'Whatever kind of word is that?' I asked him. ' "The End is at Hand, Prepare to Meet Thy Doom?" '

'It's a word of warning,' he said, 'in capital letters.'

'God help us all,' I said, though there didn't seem much point. 'He's cracked, he's gone doolally.'

'The End is Nigh,' he said.

The paint on his boards began to run.

'Come on in out of the rain,' I said. 'You'll catch your death.'

'The Wages of Sin!' he shouted.

I said, 'God, people are staring at you. Don't make yourself look ridiculous. Come and have a cup of tea.'

We sheltered under the market stalls. I ordered two teas and cheese rolls.

'Not bad,' said God. 'I like a bit o' cheese.'

'Don't change the subject,' I said. 'Now what's all this nonsense?'

'Evangelism,' he said. 'I've become an evangelist.'

'You've joined Cranks Anonymous,' I said. 'Who's going to take you seriously?'

'Somebody might,' he said. 'Try anything once, I thought. I live in hopes.'

'Not much hope in a message like that,' I said. 'It's a gospel for lost causes.'

God swallowed a mouthful of tea. Then he said, 'Lost causes—isn't that what the gospel's for?'

'Well, I know what you mean,' I said. 'But you can't join hands with that lot. You've seen 'em, traipsing up and down the High Street, dispensing gloom and parading their inadequacies. Lost souls in long overcoats.'

'You haven't got much time for them, have you?' said God.

'They're an embarrassment,' I told him. 'They get religion a bad name, and you a bad image.'

'Me?' said God. 'Do you think I ought to take some advertising

space on telly?—Art thou weary? Art thou languid? Art thou sore distressed? Consult your God-dealer now. Go. Get God-Power!'

'No need to be like that,' I said.

'It's wicked to mock the afflicted,' he said; without so much as a grin.

'You're serious,' I said. 'Are they afflicted?'

'No more than the rest of you,' he said. 'They're simple souls, needing a simple faith, believing that's all anyone else needs—a faith at least uncomplicated by the sort of theological gymnastics you get up to.'

'I can't help it,' I said.

'No more you can,' he said. 'Some see one way, some

65

another. . . . I see all ways. Some rejoice in me, some fear me, some see hope, some see judgement.'

'And some,' I said, 'don't see you at all.'

And God burst forth—'Immortal, invisible. . . .'

'Listen . . .' I said.

'In light inaccessible, hid from our eyes. . . .'

'Cut it out,' I said, 'I mean NON-EXISTENT.'

He stopped singing. 'Well, that's one way of looking at it.'

'It's not looking at it at all,' I said. 'It's atheism.'

'You and your Isms,' said God. 'They're entitled to their point of view, same as anyone else.'

I said, 'What? Don't you mind?'

'What's the use of minding?' said God. 'Wouldn't make any difference. I don't mind as long as folks are honest.'

I said, 'What's honesty got to do with it?'

'Everything,' he said. 'When folks say, Prove the existence of God—what do they want?'

'Proof?' I said.

'Nearly, but not quite,' he said. 'What they want is *facts*! If they were honest, they might allow that all they need is proof of possibility.'

'That's a bit vague, isn't it?' I said. 'What about proper evidence?'

'I don't know why I talk to you,' he said. 'I really don't. Who needs evidence? The merest possibility of my existence is all the evidence for faith anyone needs.'

'A sort of—er—working hypothesis?' I said, with a hint of sarcasm which he didn't completely ignore.

'Just the phrase I was looking for,' he said. 'A working hypothesis to keep people going till the day when the real facts are known.'

'What do you mean—the day?' I said. 'When?'

'All in good time,' he answered. 'All in good time.'

'Now that's not fair,' I said. 'People want to make sense of life here and now.'

'Well, they could if they weren't so dim,' he said.

'Dim?' I protested. 'Who are you calling dim? You made us the way we are.'

'I don't mean unintelligent,' he said, 'I mean. . . .'

'There you are,' I said, 'even you are lost for words.'

'Well, if you're so clever,' he answered sharply, 'you explain the meaning of life to me.'

So I kept quiet, didn't I? Then I said, 'What's the point anyway?'

'Now you're on to something,' he said. 'There isn't any point. Explain life, and where would hope be? Where would your aims and incentives get to?'

'Search me,' I said.

'Search me an' all,' said God. 'Search the world of possibilities, search the world of creativity, the world of challenge and imagination. . . .'

He was getting carried away again with his own eloquence, so I interrupted.

'Where's the meaning of life in all that?' I asked.

'In the *search*!' he said suddenly.

I said, 'God, you're a riddle.'

And he said to me, 'Solve it . . . I dare you.'

Interview

The interview was over, and the other candidate, like a patient about to undergo an operation, had gone into the Boardroom to have his confidence removed.

'Cup o' tea?' said a voice. It was God.

'Just the job,' I said. 'You couldn't have timed it better.'

'I've been keeping an eye on you,' he said. 'I saw you'd been in.'

'In, and through, and round and out again,' I said. 'I feel . . . processed.'

'Hard . . . cheese?' said God, grinning sheepishly. 'They asked you some good questions, though, didn't they?'

'You'd *know*, of course,' I said.

'Of course,' said God.

'I suppose you knew the answers as well,' I said. 'You could have told me a few.'

'Now, now,' said God, 'I wouldn't want folks accusing me of having favourites.' He jerked a thumb at the Boardroom door. 'Your mate in there,' he said, 'it might be his turn to get the job.'

'Turn?' I said. 'Turn? These things aren't decided in turns. They're won on merit. You know—like heaven.'

There was a long silence.

'Like hell,' said God.

'Here,' I said, 'you mind your language. They'll think it's me and I'll never get the job. Anyway, I don't believe in hell.'

'Not after all you've just been through?' he said.

'Oh, that half-hour of torture?' I said. 'I'll survive. It's hardly a lake of fire and brimstone. What's one interview compared to the everlasting flames of hell?'

'Might be the end of the world,' he suggested.

'For one of us,' I said. 'Anyway, what are the things of this world compared to the rewards of heaven?'

'Coo, hark at you,' said God. 'You do believe in heaven then—the everlasting prize for good behaviour.'

'You can't catch me out with that one,' I said. 'I know what it says in the Bible about harlots and sinners.'

'You *would*,' he said. 'Er, what does it say exactly?'

I didn't really like to tell him, but I think he knew that anyway.

'You know,' I said, 'about harlots and sinners being first in the queue.'

'First come, first served,' said God. 'It's all a question of whose need is greatest. What do folks want with heaven when they can reap satisfaction on earth? Heaven's theirs already.'

'I don't believe that either,' I said.

'You should,' he said. 'It's a thought worth encouraging.'

'Then what about the *other* story?' I asked him.

'Which one's that?' he said.

'The one about the sheep and the goats,' I said. 'You know the one. The sheep on the right, the goats on the left; and the king

welcomes the sheep into his kingdom because they've cared for their fellow men. The goats are damned to hell because they've done nothing.'

'You do know your Bible well,' said God. 'There must be a prize for that.'

I said, 'Maybe, but not in heaven it seems.'

'Ah,' said God. 'Now listen. You're right about the goats. They did nothing. You know the sort of folks they are. Keep themselves to themselves. Anything for a quiet life. Never do anyone any harm. Well, of course not—they never *do* anything!'

'Sins of omission?' I suggested.

'Maybe,' said God. 'But I don't need to worry about them, do I? They worry enough about themselves.'

'All right,' I said. 'But we're straying from the point. . . .'

71

'All we like sheep. . . .' he started.

'Never mind about that,' I said. 'What about the harlots and sinners? It isn't fair, you know. It just isn't good enough. What about all those people who've done good all their lives?'

'I keep telling you,' he said. 'They've had their share of heaven already. They ought to know better than to deprive those who've never even tasted it.'

'You're barmy.' I said. 'It's asking for trouble. You're encouraging wickedness.'

'Rubbish,' said God. 'I'm admitting that people who dare to do things expose themselves to temptation and the risk of falling. And I'm saying that forgiveness is readily available for them all. And if you know your Bible as well as you think, you'd know it was that way round. The first shall be last and the last shall be first.'

'And God helps those who help themselves,' I said.

'It doesn't say *that* anywhere,' he said.

'It's true all the same,' I answered.

And he said, 'I've yet to see a grab-all-give-nowt die with a smile on his face.'

'Do you really shut them out?' I said.

'The pity of it is,' he answered, 'until the very last second, they never even consider coming in. The door's always open, you know. Anyone who thinks it's open to some and shut to others commits the worst sin of all.'

'Pride?' I said.

And God said, 'Pride . . . I'll take your cup if you've done. Then he left, shutting the door.

I didn't get the job.

Seeing is . . .

I saw God again the other day. I *did*—sitting in church!—waiting for the service to begin.

'Fancy seeing you,' I whispered. You have to whisper in church or you might wake folks up.

'Don't be cheeky,' said God. 'You know it's where I'm supposed to be.'

I said, 'Yes, but I didn't expect to see you actually sitting there.'

'I've come to see what you're up to,' he said. 'Besides, I like a good sing now and then.'

So we looked at the numbers on the board and did a quick flick through the hymn book.

'No "Top o' the Pops" in that lot,' God said. 'Let's go for a walk.'

I said, 'What, now?'

'Why not?' he said. 'Bit o' fresh air'd do 'em all good. Come on.'

So he led the way, and several ladies in feathery hats poked wooden faces at us as we left.

'Breathe that,' said God, as we stood outside in the sunshine. 'Rain-washed grass and sky, steamy hedgerows, smell of earth and scent of blossom.'

'Very poetic,' I said. 'But what about my conscience?'

'What's the matter?' he said. 'Feeling guilty?'

I said, 'No, of course not . . . well, no, well . . . yes, I suppose that's what it is. I'm not happy, playing truant.'

'Makes you think, doesn't it,' he said. 'Finding reasons for coming out makes you look for reasons for staying in.'

'But I've always been to church,' I told him. 'I thought it's what you wanted—worship, prayer, obedience. . . .'

'Go on,' said God.

'What else *is* there?' I said.

'Well, don't you expect to get something out of it?' he asked.

'Well, yes, of course,' I said. 'Fellowship, spiritual refreshment, comfort in time of need, peace of mind. . . .'

'Oooh, that *is* lovely,' said God. 'Say it all again.'

'I'm *serious!*' I said.

'Rubbish,' said God. 'You're not even thinking. What do you expect to put into or get out of going to church when you sing nothing but sentimental, self-indulgent choruses and listen to preachers delivering second-class parcels of religious drivel?'

I said, 'Now, wait a minute. You tell *me*. If it's all such a waste of time, why do I feel so uncomfortable at not going?'

'You've breached the security of regular habit,' he said.

'And you've stuffed guilt into the gap,' I answered.

'You feel guilty at neglecting your tradition,' said God. 'I establish no traditions. They are merely the tools with which men work to find their way to me through my creation. They become blunt, and need sharpening; or they become obsolete and need replacement.'

'What are your trying to say?' I asked him. 'I don't feel safe.'

So God said, 'Go on, then. Go back in and join your friends. It's

76

somewhere to go where people think about the same things you think about, a small community where your talents can be used and appreciated. Put in a nutshell, it makes you feel wanted—boosts your ego.'

'You make it sound as though I only go to church for my own good,' I said. 'I could go to the pub or the pictures for that.'

'Now whose side are *you* on?' he said.

Well, I didn't know. 'You've got me all confused,' I said. 'You make churchgoing sound like a crime.'

'Criminals,' he said, 'take all, give nothing. It's all a matter of intent. Like anything else, from churchgoing you only get out of it as much as you put in.'

I said, 'Ahhhh—the *collection*!'

But he looked at me witheringly.

'I mean,' said God at last, 'the devotion to others of time, energy, work and leisure, of which money is a mere token.'

'But I thought church was your *special place*,' I said.

'Not if it doesn't enable you to see me in other places—the farm, the shop, the playground, the factory, the tube train, the trans-atlantic jet, the tenement block, the grimy slum, the executive suite. . . .'

'Steady on,' I said. 'Steady on. You'll do yourself an injury.'

'You may deceive yourself,' he said, 'that you've met me in church, and still pass me by in the street.'

'But I must go to church,' I said, 'or I may forget who I'm looking for.'

'My face is the face of men's needs,' said God. 'Easily recognized. They are many, and yours is amongst them. Go on. Go back in. But take care not to think that the only virtue is in what you do for others; it is also what you are trusting and humble enough to let others do for you.'

We went back in. I looked at the people, kneeling, sitting, lolling, staring—in various attitudes of prayer.

I said, 'Well, here we are, God—a bunch of ordinary human beings, with all our good intentions and all our inadequacies. What are we to do?'

He smiled. 'You know full well,' he said. 'It's all been written down for you.'

'Well?' I said.

He winked and did a little tap dance in the porch. 'I'll just nip up there and do 'em a turn,' he said.

So he stood in the pulpit, opened the heavy black Bible and read, 'Seek and you shall find, ask and you shall receive, knock and it shall be opened unto you.'

The people, with great solemnity, nodded their heads as though they had understood every word. Then he pointed a large warning finger at them and said, 'Don't ever think you have totally found me. Keep on looking.'

Trouble is, the more you get to know him, the more you wonder what he's like.